Filippo Corridoni

Monograph by

Alceste de Ambris

Translated by Richard Robinson

Sunny Lou Publishing Company
Portland, Oregon, USA
http://www.sunnyloupublishing.com

Original Publication Date: 2025 September 7

ISBN: 978-1-955392-80-8

This translation from Italian is based on the Società
Tipografica Editoriale Porta edition of *I Volontari: Filippo
Corridoni*, Piacenza, 1922.

Contents

Contents

Preface

Readers will readily understand why the pages that we present here, far from having the pretension of a rigid and cold objectivity, are keenly imbued with the fraternal affection that the biographer felt for Filippo Corridoni during the last ten years of this latter person's life; may they, therefore, forgive their markedly personal character.

The biographer nevertheless doubts his being able to convey to readers the sensation of ardent commotion with which he wrote: only someone who had the good fortune of knowing Filippo Corridoni, of loving him, and of being loved by him in turn, in the intimacy of a long friendship, can fully understand this, which the pen is unequal to the task of expressing.

For Filippo Corridoni was not only a magnificent agitator, a daring and expert leader of crowds, a heroic soldier of his faith: he was also a gentle friend, an unforgettable companion, an irresistible enchanter of souls.

We remember how, after his having visited Paris only once and for only a few days, he succeeded in leaving an indelible impression even on the coldest men of that skeptical and blasé environment, so that they continued to speak about him many months afterwards with affectionate admiration.

Whence came that singular magnetic force of attraction that he unconsciously exercised even on the most refractory and thick-skinned individuals, no less than on the crowds – anyone who has an understanding of love will perceive it, after reading the autobiographical pages that we publish below.

About Corridoni one could well repeat what Mazzini wrote of Jacopo Ruffini: "I do not find here on earth, among those who have a concept of faith and constancy of sacrifice, anyone quite like you."

Filippo Corridoni was, in fact, one of those privileged beings who sum up and sublimate in a complete individual synthesis the noblest virtues of the stirp and generation to which they belong.

Even in the best [individuals], the sincerity of conviction is sometimes lightly tinged by doubt, the will to sacrifice restrained by hesitation, the depth of faith clouded by human weakness. In Corridoni this never happened. He had effortlessly reached the absolute, because his exceptional nature brought him there.

Saint Catherine said: "*Et si religio jusserit signemus fidem sanguine.*"[1] Filippo Corridoni did not even allow for the hypothetical. For him, to affirm the faith with blood was not an eventuality: it was a categorical commandment, a precise duty.

Perchance it was this by-now tranquil certainty of sacrifice that permitted him to conserve, in the midst of the bitterest trials, that admirable serenity, that fresh, youthful joy that made him so dear to all who knew him, like an extremely rare gift in men

---

[1]*Et si religio...*: Latin for "And if religion should command, let us sign our faith in blood."

whose life is an ongoing struggle.

And yet, whoever believed that the concept of a superior duty in Filippo Corridoni was the cause or effect of a blind fanaticism of irrational impetuosity, or of a sentimental unilateralism unsupported by the necessary knowledge of actual facts and their relativity, would fall into a gross error.

Like all those whom the continual urgencies of action grant no leisure for calm reflection, Corridoni never found the time to document in books what his inordinately lively intellect, matured by more than ten years of experience, could have produced. The manifestations of thought that he left are almost all fragmentary: newspaper articles, conference reports, letters... His admirable speeches, always extemporaneous, were collected, but only in hurried, colorless, and insignificant summaries. And it is no longer possible to reconstruct them.

The most complete work he wrote consists of scarcely 113 pages written during his stay in prison in April, 1915: a small number of pages, then, but which in their concision possess so much originality of thought and acuteness of observation as to serve as the outline for a thick volume.

Those pages, which, given the date on which they were written, barely seven months before his death, may be regarded as his definitive thought, meditated and measured like a testament; they demonstrate that the enthusiastic inspirer of crowds, the ardent combatant who was ready to sacrifice himself, was also a formidable thinker, endowed with a rare learning that was enlivened by an exceptionally lucid intelligence and by a free and ample vision of the national and social problem.

In the sad and reflective silence of the prison cell, he who was preparing to offer himself as a sacred holocaust to the Fatherland of his immaculate youth saw the future course of history with astonishing clarity.

Certain pages of his have the quality of prophecy, ruthlessly confirmed today by events. And yet, even in the face of a clear perception of the true worth and non-decisive results of the sacrifice that he prepared himself for, he – voluntary offering – remained steadfast in accepting the war with an ardent will, inspiring unprecedented heroism.

Given that Corridoni was so self-assured and superior to every human weakness, he had no need even for the comfort of a great illusion to wrap himself in, as he set about fulfilling the supreme duty that he had freely chosen. Nor did he reject the cold, objective truth, or seek to delude himself by comparing the anticipated result with the greatness of the sacrifice he was preparing to make. He knew, and he said as much, that war could only yield results that were far inferior to those that a flattering and fallacious hope left room to imagine. And yet, he went serenely to war.

Corridoni has, for this reason, left us – together with his unforgettable memory – a great lesson that we must learn to treasure: when faced with recognized necessities, however harsh – for the fullness of the struggle indispensable to the life and freedom of a people, a class, or an individual – one must never lose heart in disappointed dejection; rather, we must draw from the harshness of the necessities that confront us a reason to press forward more rapidly with our work.

To his memory, then, we intend to pay a threefold homage, without in any way concealing the frankness of our thought. If those who read us possess – as we believe [they do] – a nobility of sentiment, whatever their political or social convictions, they will understand why we did not wish to mutilate Corridoni by speaking only of the Interventionist and the Volunteer. Even the Revolutionary must be understood and admired by Italians who sincerely wish to honor the memory of both the Inspirer and Hero, for it was precisely on the soil of Filippo Corridoni's revolutionary faith that the crimson flower of his sacrifice for the Fatherland blossomed [so] magnificently.

– Alceste de Ambris

The Revolutionary

The Revolutionary

In the Burning Bush

I met Filippo Corridoni for the first time in person during the memorable agrarian strike of Parma in 1908.

At the beginning of the movement, he found himself in Nice where he had taken refuge to escape the consequences of a sentence of several years of imprisonment, given to him in Milan for antimilitarism. When the struggle was at its height, we saw him descend upon Parma, under the name of "Leo Cervisio," with his boyish smile, wearing a pair of trousers too short for him.

In that period, the trousers Pippo wore – thus did his friends call him – were always too short. He was growing at a vertiginous rate. The tailor had barely finished fashioning a suit for him when already he had outgrown it. Only several years later did Pippo finally stop growing – thank Heaven! – and his trousers were no longer too short; but his face always wore that ingenuous smile of before.

We tried to make "Leo Cervisio" understand all the dangers that he was exposing himself to – in his legal situation – by participating in a struggle that was becoming more acrimonious with each passing day. There was no chance of persuading him. He wanted to remain, at all costs, in that burning bush, exposing himself more than any other, with that tranquil and cheerful insolence which made him dearer every day. The police, moreover, never suspected that "Leo Cervisio" was the condemned Filippo Corridoni. Arrested multiple times, he was always released without the police suspecting that they had caught so terrible a delinquent.

On June 20, 1908, when, by Giolitti's command, the Chamber of Labor of Parma was assaulted, he was on the street to defend it. A cavalry officer, who was charging at the crowd at the head of a platoon, pointed a pistol at him, crying:

"Clear off, or I'll shoot!"

"Leon Cervisio" did not move. Alone and unarmed, he responded by offering him his chest:

"Shoot then, coward!"

The officer – who was certainly not a coward – taken aback by such heroic audacity, did not fire. Meanwhile a band of young men arrived who pushed the platoon back under a cloud of stones and dragged their temerarious companion along with, saving him through the alleyways of Oltretorrente, the well-known proletarian and subversive quarter of Parma, which was then poised to supply numerous volunteers to the war.

That same evening Corridoni found himself with me in an large underground room in Borgo dei Grassani.[2] There were several others as well, all in-

___
[2]Borgo dei Grassani: a suburb of Parma.

duced to take refuge there from the police hunt underway for all those suspected of having participated in the organization of the strike, which they were determined to crush at all costs. The statal violence raged through the streets of Parma: rapid bursts of gunfire, arrest warrants. No one could be sure that he would not, at any moment, be shot in the stomach or seized by the hair as a member of the *criminal association*, a charge invented by the fervid fantasy of the functionaries for public safety, to provide a legal pretext for performing arrests *en masse*.

The next day – secure in the knowledge that the arrest warrant applied only to me – my companions exited from our place of refuge. With them also exited "Leo Cervisio" who remained active in the province hit by the severest reaction for another month still, until the hypocritical accusation of his being a scoundrel posing as a Socialist constrained him to go into exile again, in which [state] I continued to find myself. He came to greet me in Lugano, while passing through; and a couple of months later I found him in Zurich. It was a sad and wet October. Corridoni made a living as an assistant to bricklayers. Worn out by toil, sickly, reduced to the most dire poverty, with his trousers shorter than ever, he continued to smile that beautiful and serene smile of his, and his eyes sparkled with a secure, ardent, and joyful faith, just as in the finest moments of the struggles that we had fought together.

Autobiographical Pages

Corridoni's biography was sketched out by himself in a letter addressed to a person dear to him, shortly before his death on the battlefield. Nothing is more moving than the simple and candid prose of the pages in the document before me, which I reproduce in full:

> *I am not yet twenty-eight years old. My parents are laborers and now live in modest comfort, the fruit of their constant effort. I attended an upper vocational school, from which I graduated with a diploma as a mechanical expert. I came to Milan in 1905 and practiced the profession of draftsman and machine designer until 1907. From the Republican ideals of my early childhood, I became a revolutionary Socialist within the first few months of my stay in this city. I joined the subversive militia in the spring of 1906 and my youthful ardor together with a certain liveliness of intellect led me at once to the front ranks.*
>
> *In January of 1907, I was Secretary of the Socialist Youth Circle; in March, founder of [the journal]* Rompete Le File[3] *together with Maria Rigier.[4] The following April I was Vice Secretary of*

[3] *Rompete le File*: Break the Ranks.

[4] Rigier: also spelt Rygier.

the Provincial Socialist Federation. At that time, I was pure in soul and senses; I did not love women; nor wine; nor meat. I saved a lot and spent very little, so as to be able to devote the greater part of my wages to my ideas. But a ferocious, implacable persecution by the police was soon raised against me, which only stopped at the doorstep of the caserne, and which will probably continue to pursue me once I have laid aside the soldier's uniform, unless... the Austrians can provide some remedy.

In May 1907, I received my first sentence; and since then I must have accumulated a good thirty. For eight consecutive years, my life has been extremely harsh, and terrible. I have uninterruptedly gone from one prison to another, with several periods of exile in between.

I have suffered, and greatly, but I have the supreme pride of being able to attest before the universe, and without fear of refutation, that my days of suffering have been supported by me with courage and equanimity, without anyone being able to accuse me to my face of one instance of weakness or cowardice.

I have suffered hunger, cold, derision,

vituperation, and mortification, without speaking of my suffering to anyone. I have worked at every trade, during my painful exile, from bricklayers' assistant to the seller of chestnuts. I have survived for months on simple bread and Roman ricotta, or on a plate of spaghetti costing four cents, eating one meal a day. And yet, despite all that, here I am with my faith intact, ready to take up, once again, the way of the cross for the triumph of my immortal ideas.

In these eight years, I have carried my message from one corner of Italy to the other; everywhere, I have made friends; perhaps also some adversaries: but no enemies. No enemies because (and this is not a virtue) my soul is incapable of hatred. Or rather, I hate evil itself but not the people who commit it. And if I fight an adversary, even with asperity and roughness, I do it to heal him of his moral evil, and not for the pleasure of seeing him humiliated or vanquished. Despite my pencil, sharp like a sword, my arms are always open, ready to embrace any adversary who repents and believes again.

My ideas bring me nothing but prison and poverty; but if prison tempers me for future battles, if prison nourishes my soul and intellect, poverty fills me with pride. If I had the soul of a speculator or if I had compromised my conscience for a single moment, I would now enjoy an enviable economic position. But as I know, and feel, that an illicitly earned wage would weigh on me as a mortal remorse, and abase me in my own eyes to the point of spiritual death, I can calmly say that poverty will be the inseparable companion of my not-long life...

For ten years now, my adversaries have succeeded in spreading all manner of injurious stories about me, interwoven with foolish gossip. I have never felt the need to respond to such filth, in that the truth will always out, naturally, and such gentlemen have brought summary justice on their own heads for their base acts. I too have my faults – who does not? – but the efforts I have made for so many years now in order to cleanse my soul of every impurity and to make myself worthy of the mission that destiny has entrusted to me, have succeeded in making me into a man who can walk anywhere in the world without fear of blushing or lowering his gaze before anyone.

Concept of Life

In another letter, also written from the front, he repeated the moral principle that had always inspired
his life, with these words:

> *I have loved my ideas more than a
> mother, more than any beloved mis-
> tress, more than life.*

> *I have always served them ardently,
> devoutly, and in poverty. For I have
> also loved poverty, like Saint Francis
> of Assisi and Fra Jacopone [da Todi],
> convinced that a contempt for riches is
> the best and most tempered hauberk
> for a revolutionary.*

> *I have always sought to adapt my life
> to the moral dictates of my doctrine:
> while I have not always succeeded,
> since the flesh is weak, I am proud to
> assert that my effort has been sincere
> and constant.*

> *If destiny allows it, I will die without
> having hated anyone – not even the
> Austrians – with only one great regret:
> that I was unable to give all my ener-
> gy, which I still feel inside me, to the
> cause of the workers; but with one
> great satisfaction: that I have always
> obeyed the will of my conscience.*

That is more than enough, I believe, to delineate the spiritual figure of the revolutionary who volunteered for the Fatherland in the hour of greatest danger.

Filippo Corridoni's physical appearance harmonized perfectly with the spiritual one. Tall, slender, blond, with big, bright, and exceptionally gentle eyes, rosy-cheeked and smiling even at the saddest and most tragic moments, he exercised a singular charm on the people who were near him, on the crowds whom he led into the bitterest of battles, lifting them by his example to a comprehension of the ideal beauty of sacrifice that asks for no reward.

People and crowds intuited in him an absolute sincerity, a nobility of soul without shadows or rifts, an extremely delicate humanity that bitter experience could not diminish; just as the hardships of a life of poverty and suffering could not efface the youthful freshness of his physique, on which not even illness seemed capable of leaving a trace.

The Interventionist

The Interventionist

Hearth of Faith

When the Great War broke out, Filippo Corridoni found himself in prison, for one of the usual legal shenanigans whereby the police deluded themselves into [believing they were] "driving some sense into him."

Corridoni was, at that time, at the head of the Syndicalist Union of Milan, and I – having returned from exile the year before – shared living quarters with him in a modest "pensione" on the fourth floor of a building on via Eustachi, in a new neighborhood between Porta Venezia and Loreto. In addition to Corridoni and me, Attilio Deffenu – a small Sardinian, who also died heroically at the front, while fighting with the Sassari Brigade – Michele Bianchi, Cesare Rossi, and my brother Amilcare, a comrade of Corridoni's in the leadership of the Syndicalist Union of Milan – all shared a table at the "pensione."

It was a revolutionary circle or cenacle, the "pensione" was, on via Eustachi, and it did not lack character. The political homogeneity of those who composed it did not exclude the most profound individual differences. But among those men of all races and all temperaments, who were united in a common ideal, a friendship flourished, so sincere and fraternal as to exclude even – something extremely rare in po-

litical cenacles – petty jealousies, malice, and recipro-
cal backbiting.

I, who had the good fortune to be able to par-
ticipate in that group until the war came along and
dissolved it, cannot think back without strong emo-
tions on that "pensione" of via Eustachi. Poor "pensione," having fallen silent and become empty by the
end of May 1915: whereas formerly it was so full of
fervor, working enthusiasm, rich discussions, friendly
altercations, voices, and laughter!

It was like a little slipway or airstrip for international or Italian revolutionary syndicalism. Very
few of the most well-known agitators had not visited
that eating room of the "pensione" on via Eustachi or
taken a seat at that table. Not to mention, among the
deceased: Vidali visited us, who brought with him the
nostalgia of his Trieste; Chiasserini, still formally
bound to the Socialist party, but in spirit and in work
entirely one with us; Reguzzoni, fervid with life;
Rabolini, with the face of a little girl, sweet mask of
heroic will; Peppino and Baldino, Corridoni's two
brothers; the modest and valiant Luigi Maltoni, from
an area in Romagna with a name evocative of merid-
ional luminosity: Terra del Sole...

All these whom I have mentioned fell in the
the Great War, wearing the uniform of an Italian volunteer. As for the others who passed into that little
room of the "pensione" on via Eustachi, it is impossi-
ble to remember them all. Even from abroad, the
guests arrived: Frenchmen, Belgians, Englishmen,
Russians... There were even Armenians and Hungari-
ans.

At times – or, it would be more accurate to say: often enough – around the table that welcomed us twice a day, there was some place that remained empty for many long weeks. For the most part, it was Filippo Corridoni's; but others, from time to time, were also absent: it had to do with more or less brief visits... to the Slammer. And yet, despite these sadnesses, despite the fervor of the struggles that we were engaged in, the snares that we sensed around us, the dangers of every sort that unremittingly menaced us – we were cheerful and full of life, ready to enjoy what little pleasure life offered us, in the extreme modesty of our economic conditions, between one battle and the next, between one stint in prison and another in exile. We were all young, but already veterans of the most bitter struggles that were being fought at that time; and it seemed to us that a dark foreboding encouraged us to seize each brief moment of joy with the avid haste of those who would not live past tomorrow: "Whoever would be happy should be – for of tomorrow there is no certainty," was oft repeated by Corridoni who gladly filled the "pensione" with his fresh, resounding bursts of laughter and "yet a slight melancholy often veiled his eyes, as if the shadow of the future and death, unknown even to himself, was extending over his soul."

War

The assassination in Sarajevo came, and then – with a rapid collapse which the International, which we believed in, did not even attempt to slow down – the war! I had spent two weeks of hell after the barbaric invasion of Belgium, while in my soul the ideologies that I had believed in up until then were atrociously clashing with the tremendous reality that shattered them under the inexorable thrust of the German bayonets. I resolved finally to say out loud what my conscience dictated to me, seizing the occasion of an invitation sent to me by the Syndicalist Union of Milan to speak on "The Proletariat and the War."

On the eve of the conference, I confided in my companions at the "pensione": "Tomorrow" I said, "I will say things that perhaps will put me against the entire labor movement. But that is the least of my worries: it would pain me far more if I had a rupture with you all too..."

My companions at the pensione – who were all present, except Corridoni who had been arrested, as I have already said, for one of the usual legal shenanigans – promised me that they would not miss the conference. That evening we ate in silence, heavy in sorrow. My companions intuited what I would say, which they were thinking as well, but did not dare to confess. Everyone had the sensation of finding himself at one of those decisive moments in life that are heavy on the heart. It was our entire past, the idol to which we had sacrificed our entire youth, which we were preparing to smash with our iconoclastic hands. And there also loomed the anguished apprehension that our fraternal friendship, cemented by the constant cooperation of intentions and work, might go to pieces in the crash of that tragic moment.

The next evening we were happy to find our-selves together again, spiritually united as before. My companions had listened to my talk attentively, without finding any essential point of dissension in the case that I made, of the necessity of Italian intervention in the Great War. Everyone was in agreement in recognizing that we could not and must not keep silent about what our conscience as men and revolutionaries imposed on us to proclaim as a hard truth.

The joy of our confirmed union of spirits was disturbed by one doubt alone: What would Corridoni have said? Corridoni, so fervid and so absolutely convinced in his antimilitarism, Corridoni who could rightly feel exasperated by his recent most iniquitous arrest, Corridoni isolated behind bars, which are difficultly penetrated by the current of ideas, because the events that determine them are unknown or poorly known by those who are locked up – would Corridoni have understood our stance? Or would we not perhaps find him against us, with all his combative vigor, with that enormous strength of will and influence that he exerts on the crowd, with that well-known capacity in him to fight and to sacrifice as soon as he was released?

That doubt continued to torment us so much so that it was decided to have a conversation with Corridoni at once, in order to know his thoughts. Deffenu and I were charged with visiting him in the clinker. I still remember, as if it were yesterday, the commotion that filled us when, at our rather cautious hints, Corridoni burst into one of those big beautiful laughs of his, making fun of our diplomacy and declaring himself completely in agreement with us.

"Yes, the war is a national and revolutionary duty. Yes, we have to want it and wage it, as soon as Italy enters the field..."

Corridoni said this in the gloomy visiting room, under the vigilant eyes of the guard. But behind bars, where he was unjustly suffering, he had already prepared himself for the sacrifice. His youth was the holocaust that he offered up to the step-motherly Fatherland, generous to him only in persecutions and hunger.

The Campaign for Intervention

As soon as he got out of prison, Corridoni threw himself into the furious struggle already initiated by Italy's intervention. He threw himself into it as only he knew how, without missing a beat and without restraint, with all the force of his enthusiasm and with absolute faith, with an ardor of sacrifice that prefigured the extreme sacrifice he had vowed for himself.

Attilio Deffenu, commemorating him several days after his death, wrote the following:

> It was unforgettable, the tempestuous rally at the Arte Moderna [gallery], toward the end of November 1914, where the matter of revolutionary interventionism was presented in all sin-

cerity before the perplexed conscience of the working class; but what many do not know, except a few intimate friends, is an episode that I am compelled to recall. On the afternoon of the day set for the rally, Corridoni received a telegram from his family wherein an unexpected worsening of his mother's ill-health was announced: she seemed close to death. The blow was terrible: but the rally had been scheduled: to fail to show up could seem like an act of cowardice; to be sure, it meant exposing himself to the perfidious and maligning criticism of the neutralist opposition. But he went, and it is easy to imagine with what a state of mind: he spoke, as only he knew how and could, with a lofty and moving eloquence, drowning out the rabid hurlings of the Socialists in [Bernhard von] Bülow's pay, and succeeding, notwithstanding the organized obstructionism, to make himself heard and applauded. At a certain point, I remember, he began to explain by what reasoning, despite an unshakeable faith in the International, he felt that he could not renounce the fatherland, or the countryside where he had been born, where the sweet dialect of his mother was spoken...

"Federzoni!"[5] This tendentious invective, aimed at denaturing the high-minded sentiment that moved Corridoni and at depicting him as a traitor to the revolutionary syndicalist cause that he loved above all else, rang out in the hall streaked with flashes of ire, flushed red with the eruptive fire of passions.

He turned toward the small group of agitated men and uttered not a word. But those who were near him saw a tear fall down his cheek, saw him swallow it in silence, painfully, and 'felt' that his thought had turned to his distant mother who perhaps at that very moment was agonizing on her bed of suffering...

In February of this year (1915) he was arrested again on the train, under the imputation of an infraction of the press, while he was on his way to Treviso to hold a conference there in favor of intervention. And from prison he wrote to me on February 24: "I see that your propaganda for intervention is incessant. I am particularly happy

---

[5]Federzoni: In reference to Luigi Federzoni (AD 1878-1967), an Italian statesman and writer who was originally a nationalist and was also an early advocate for Italy's intervention in WWI. He later mediated between Vittorio Emanuelle III and Mussolini during the March on Rome and was President of the Senate from 1929 to 1939.

*to hear it. The neutralists will un-
doubtedly have profited by my arrest,
crying out that in Italy freedom is tam-
pered with more than in Austria, etc.
Tell them that as long as I am treated
in the German fashion, I will always
shout 'Love live the war!' and that
they will need to do much better than
these little miseries to shake my profound and deeply-rooted conviction
that it is only through defeat of the
central empires that Europe can be
dragged toward a greater and more
solid freedom."*

In March, after a trial at the [Court of] Assize, he regained his freedom and returned to the interventionist battle with a vigor that prison seemed to have renewed.

Who does not remember the magnificent work of Corridoni, culminating in the days of May 1915, when the neutralist resistance was swept away in a wave of passion? In those memorable days, Corridoni was truly the master of Milan. The piazzas and the streets where his. His words kindled flames of enthusiasm, his person and his gesture[6] carried the crowds to the ultimate heights of heroic volition.

Many there are, certainly, who worked tirelessly for the intervention; but there is no one in Italy

---

[6]gesture: For an idea of the "gesture," see the photograph of Corridonni on the back cover of this book. One has to wonder how much of this gesture influenced, later, Mussolini, who can be seen in the same photograph.

who can say that he gave more to the Cause than Filippo Corridoni did. Corridoni did not merely offer
himself, his indefatigable effort, his pure youth: he offered also the popularity that he had won in eight
years of indefatigable toil, by means of renunciations
and unspeakable suffering. Everything was consumed
on the altar of the Fatherland as seen through the eyes
of a filial son in the hour of pain and sorrow – by him
who had known the Fatherland only in the odious
guise of persecuting policemen and iniquitous judges.

The Volunteer

The Volunteer

In the Caserne and at the Front

No sooner had the hard struggle attained its goal and war was finally declared than the "pensione" of via Eustachi became empty. The small room where we gathered twice a day for modest meals and deafening discussions fell silent. All the table companions of the "pensione" had enlisted as volunteers in order to fight the war that they had preached: first among them, Filippo Corridoni.

I remember him – it was the last time I saw him – standing in the eating room of the "pensione": he was wearing the outfit of a soldier, and he was laughing at his shoes which were too large and at his pants which were too short. We had a brief chat. I also needed to get myself to the storehouse of my regiment. We embraced and kissed each others' cheeks, our eyes filled with tears. Departing, I carried with me the despairing certitude that I would never see Filippo Corridoni again.

This certitude was, moreover, shared by all those who knew his temerarious audacity and his firm intention of offering, with the holocaust of his life, a memorable example.

At this point, I believe it is my duty to leave the word to someone who was always beside him during the entire campaign of the war, from the time when, in the vast Caserne of via Lamarmora, he practiced marching with his fellow soldiers and gave an attentive ear to the instructions of officers or non-commissioned officers unto the day of his glorious death!

Dino Roberto, his comrade in arms wrote:

He was the most disciplined soldier in the caserne. His one and only aspiration was to get to the front as early as possible. I remember that every day spent in the caserne without useful exercises or practical instruction put him in a bad mood, and not a few times he protested in a loud voice against a supposed obstructionism that made the military preparation of volunteers slow and tedious.

When we first learned of the order of departure for the theater of war, no one showed more joy than he did.[7]

On the evening of July 25, more than

---

[7]Original footnote: On the eve of his departure, Corridoni, to the organized workers of the Syndicalist Union of Milan whom he had rallied to interventionism, addressed the following greeting, in which the purest syndicalist faith is combined with a most devout love for the Fatherland:

At this moment of departure for the field of honor and glory, I feel the imperious need to address to you, brave companions of the recent battles of yesterday, my affectionate and fervid greeting.

*one hundred thousand cheering Mi-
lanese lined his passage, while, with
eyes gleaming with joy and a smile on
his lips, he set out for the new Italian
lands that were later to bear witness
to his valor and his martyrdom.*

This ought to give you an indication of my unaltered and unalterable affection for our beloved institution, the unbreakable bulwark of workers' rights, and also the certainty of seeing you all steadfast and unwavering around the immaculate battle flag, on the day when fortune leads me back to you, safe and sound, in order to take up again, with your trust, my place in the fight.

How fiercely proud I am of you, o comrades of the Syndicalist Union! You, first and almost alone, understood from the very first months of this year of passion what Italy's duty was, and, with your solidarity and steadfastness of intention and action, you frustrated the plans of perverting our proletariat, ignobly attempted by the official [cadres of] Socialism.

You felt that the cause of martyred Belgium, of trampled France, of agonizing Serbia, of menaced England, was our cause, and, as active and effective Internationalists, as enlightened antimilitarists, you accepted the war of our and others' liberation.

And now, wage war! Our glorious organization has the honor and pride of having 80 percent of our associates in the ranks of the army, of whom 500 volunteers.

They fight as valiants, that much is indubitable; but they demand of you, their comrades, that you maintain a steadfast and resolute attitude in both good and adverse fortune. They demand, above all, that the energies of

The crowd, hastening to celebrate the volunteers, encapsulated its trembling salute to the departing young men in a cry of "Viva Corridoni!" thus lifting him in its infallible perception to the ideal symbol of the spirit of sacrifice which they showed themselves imbued with.

Having arrived at the new regiment, which in those days was at rest, he was taken with the fever of immediate action, and obtained, together with a few others, [permission] to go at once to fight in another regiment which then found itself at the front line.

---

especially you, o metallurgic comrades, be utilized in one supreme goal: victory.

We at the front, you in the workshops, we all have a serious and noble duty to absolve, for the good fortune of Italy, for the freedom of Europe, for the future of Humanity.

Comrades of labor, act so that, once victory is achieved, when we resume the struggle of our faith – today more alive in our hearts than yesterday – it may be said by our class competitors themselves that you deserve the realization of your dreams for a better future because of the sincerity, enthusiasm, and ardor with which you fight all your battles, whether they be for the fatherland, humanity, or the sacred rights of your labor.

Long live Italy! Long life the Syndicalist Union!

— FILIPPO CORRIDONI

There, it did not take long for the officers to appreciate his exceptional qualities and entrust him with the most delicate and perilous tasks.

It was in that period of our existence at war that he experienced the greatest moral satisfaction that a simple soldier could desire. The colonel loved him like a son and held him in high esteem.

The commanding captain of the battalion that we were attached to availed himself of his work and ours for explorations, reconnaissances, and the survey of enemy positions, and in this task he excelled by his very keen intuition and promptness of intellect.

When we had to leave that regiment to return to our own, which had called us back, first the captain, then the colonel, and finally the commanding general of the brigade, when dismissing us, had nothing but words of praise for everyone, but particularly for him. In addition, they had proposed a decoration for bravery for the two deceased, Guarini and Reguzzoni, together with Corridoni and the writer, and a solemn encomium for all the others.

Several days later, our captain, pro-

*moted major, for merit in the war, ad-
dressed the following card to us:*

> *To Mr. Corridoni and Mr.
> Roberto,*
>
> *Infinite thanks especially to
> You and Roberto, but also to
> the other volunteers, whom I
> had the good fortune and plea-
> sure to have under my com-
> mand.*
>
> *I add, moreover, my feelings of
> gratitude for the sagacious
> work and intelligent contribu-
> tion furnished to me [by you]
> in the various contingencies of
> service during the war.*
>
> *– Major Figliolini.*

*When we returned to the trenches, we
were entrusted with handling the first
light cannon to be tested on the front. I
remember, as if it were only yesterday,
the thrill we felt on the evening we
fired our first shot. We had worked all
day to prepare its emplacement, and
to build the shelters of defense. As it
was getting dark, Corridoni and I, after positioning and loading the
weapon, went up to the firing line our-
selves to see what effect the shot had.*

When, from the loopholes of our de-

fense, we saw the first bomb explode squarely over enemy lines, Corridoni's enthusiasm knew no bounds.

He embraced me and kissed me on both cheeks with rapture, and from that evening on he never left his light cannon's side.

The next evening, the Austrians – who had evidently identified the position from which our bomb launcher was firing its fatal blows – responded to the first projectile sent by Corridoni, with a volley of grenades, which came and exploded just a few meters away from us, covering us in stones and dirt. We responded in turn with another well-placed bomb, but the furious hail of grenades and shrapnel that the Germans, immediately afterwards, rained down on us made us realize that these gentlemen really had it out for us, and it persuaded us to change our position in all possible haste. Which was done under Corridoni's direction without loss of men or materiel.

What it cost Filippo Corridoni to fulfill the duty he had voluntarily elected – he who had a soul that was so gentle and so yearning for freedom – we understand from a letter he had written to a dear person, on September 12,

1915; a letter of great interest also because in it he succinctly explains the reasons for which – although an antimilitarist – he had become a volunteer soldier, and the hopes he had in his heart when he fought:

... if, for a man of ordinary, average, or mediocre sensibility, war is an atrocious thing, for someone who has a high sensibility and a heart taught to feel compassion for every human misfortune, war is the most horrendous thing that a perverse mind of evil genius could think up.

Well then, I must live it, the war; for my preachings of last May, I have duties higher than any other, and my mission will require me to turn my heart to stone, guard my feelings, master every weakness, suppress every repulsion, so as to be ever ready to tell others the word that encourages, the invective that incites, the warm exhortation that keeps everyone on the bitter and difficult path of painful, but sacred duty.

Oh, the suffering, the hard-

ships, the always new dangers, I swear to you... have not encroached on my spirit [which is] steeled for difficult struggles, and the icy wing of doubt or repentance will never attenuate the heat of my convictions, which reside in the deepest recesses of my brain and heart; but the reality [of war], so horrible and terrible, has thus sharpened my sensibilities as to make me feel every joy and every sorrow multiplied a hundredfold in their essence. It is as if I had been flayed alive and every contact happened on my raw flesh rather than on the less sensible skin.

Those, then, are the reasons for my indolence. And since your eloquent appeal has been a lash to my blood and to my intellect, on the eve of retaking the path of the hill where Italian youth nobly sows the fragments of its flesh, spills its red blood in rivers, and reaps glory and death, I say to you, oh noblest of friends, at this juncture when my whole being seems to expand and unfold like a rose in the July sun, [that] all my faith today, more than ever, [is] pure like water from a source.

Devoted and enthusiastic soldier of this war, I hate it with all the strength of my soul. But I fight because I believe that this war, if it leads to the defeat of Austria and Germany, nations essentially militaristic and of a reactionary political structure, will have the same value as a great revolution and will end the era of wars of conquest for all Europe.

This war, by retaking our natural boundaries and giving us an inviolable frontier, will inevitably bring Italy to disarmament and to the redirection of military expenditures for public works, in order to favor industrial and commercial initiatives, the sole founts of wealth and national wellbeing.

The inevitable advent in the world of economic liberalism, given our abundance of highly intelligent and extremely versatile manual labor, our happy spirit of initiative, our magnificent geographic position –

*Italy is like a bridge between
Europe and Africa and is the
nation nearest to all the great
Asiatic markets – will lead us
to a rapid enrichment and to a
more rational exploitation of
our economic energies.*

*National enrichment, leading
to a celeritous industrial and
commercial development, and
proletarianizing the workers
from one end of Italy to the
other, will create the conditions necessary for a natural
interplay of class conflicts,
eliminating the false Socialism
of cooperativists, mutualists,
and petty politickers; and it
will inevitably lead to the triumph of syndicalism.*

Attack!

We do not plan to go on indefinitely about the various
episodes and campaigns fought by Corridoni as an in-
fantryman. We come, instead, to the heroic conclu-
sion of his noble life, leaving, once again, the word to
his comrade in arms, Dino Roberto:

*When the regiment was relieved, and
it passed once again behind the lines,*

Corridoni, exhausted by the long labors endured under unfavorable climatic conditions, left the trench feverish. Despite every exhortation, he decided against visiting the medic until he could no longer stand on two feet. In addition to the general state of physical deterioration, he was tormented by a malignant phlegmon that had developed from the humidity absorbed during the two weeks in the trench, spent under a constant rain. A surgical intervention was necessary, and Corridoni was required to recover in a field hospital. But he didn't wish to remain there for long. Three days after the operation, he returned to the hayloft where we had taken up lodgings, not yet recovered from the fever nor from the phlegmon.

When orders came for the regiment to move out, in order to take part in the general advance of last October (1915), the medic ordered him to return to the hospital, since he was in no condition to support the hardships and perils of the trench.

He refused to obey, and came with us.

He subjected himself to the torment of a long march with a heavy rucksack on his shoulders, and never once grumbled to anyone about the fatigue

*and the pain! Nor did he want anyone
to help him in any way.*

*When we arrived in Fogliano, where
we spent the night on the 21st and the
22nd of October, he was exhausted! He
rested for a few hours on the floor of a
vast building used for the occasion of
sheltering troops; then he had his
dressing changed.*

*In the afternoon of the 22nd, we left
Fogliano to take up positions at
Castelnuovo. We spent the night in a
trench behind the second line, and, on
the morning of the 23rd, under enemy
artillery fire, we reached our ad-
vanced positions. We arranged our-
selves in battle formation, ready for
the command to advance. Corridoni,
calm and smiling as always, spent the
morning uplifting the spirits of the
most timid among us, inciting everyone to perform their duty with courage
and self-abnegation.*

*Meanwhile, our own artillery, with
deadly accuracy, demolished piece by
piece the barbed wire fences that the
Austrians had placed to protect the
trench that we were to take by assault.
At 3 p.m. the order came to stand
ready. A half hour later a curt command rang out: "Forward!" We
bounded forward from our repair, in*

silence; our rifles armed with bayo-
nets were held firmly in our grasp.
Hunched over, but rapidly, we de-
voured the space under the murderous
fire of machine guns and the crackle
and pop of enemy rifles. The machine
gun fire made a massacre, but we did
not pause or turn back. I was beside
Corridoni; near me, smiling and tran-
quil, Rabolini ran on elastic heels, fol-
lowed by Mercanti, Gamberini, Pan-
dolfini, Major-Captain Serdillo, and
others whose names I forget.

With the barbed wire fences behind us,
contorted and torn apart by the shells,
we plunged into the trench. The few
enemy combatants that had remained
were soon put to flight by a furious
charge of bayonets. Many fell under
our thrust, while others surrendered.
But we also suffered very heavy losses.
The heroic Rabolini, having no sooner
set foot in the trench, was struck down
by a bullet to the back of his head. The
Major-Captain Signorini and two sol-
diers, struck squarely by a grenade,
lay on the ground in pieces; others,
wounded, pulled back, bleeding, while
the violent fray went on around us.
Corridoni and I, always close, at the
head of a group of brave soldiers, ran
in pursuit after the fleeing Austrians,
but we were forced to halt by a ma-

chine gun that fired on our flanks.

Death

After we pulled back to the repair of the trench now in our possession, we saw a column of enemy soldiers descending a slope on our left. They were about thirty men, and they were walking in single file along a very narrow, enclosed communication trench which put them in communication with the various dugouts making up the trench. Corridoni, who had remained with me behind the rocks to cover the others' retreat, sounded the alarm, and pointed his rifle at the enemies who were advancing at less than 150 meters away. But the shot did not leave his gun. His rifle had jammed. I leveled my weapon in turn and fired. Successively, under my shots, two Austrians fell. The rest of them, dismayed by the fate of the first, fled. We returned to our trench then, where it was urgent that we organize our defense. We were without officers; our munitions were running low, and the enemy fire was mowing us down. In the position we had won, few men held their ground in the face of enemy counterat-

tacks that ensued simultaneously at the center and on the sides.

Together with Corridoni and the Major-Captain Serdillo, we decided to assume command of the section of trench already conquered by us, which bordered on the left a position still held by the Austrians, and on the right a wide exposed passage for troops crossed horizontally by a section of barbed wire fence that the artillery had torn up or knocked down. On the other side of this exposed passage, another company of ours occupied a continuation of enemy entrenchment. The Austrians, who had noted the gap between one company of ours and the other, attempted to drive a wedge between us, to encircle us and annihilate us. Corridoni, at the head of about twenty men assumed the task of holding the right. I, with roughly the same number of men, organized the resistance on the left, while in the center, the remainder, spurred on and encouraged by the example of other volunteers and by the Major-Captain Serdillo, confronted the attacking enemy.

Meanwhile, reinforcements were urgently needed, and the volunteer Gamberini was sent to ask for them. Muni-

tions were also running low and we were forced to use the weapons abandoned by the enemy, together with their munitions, which were plentiful in the trench we had captured. When the reinforcements arrived, the gap on the right was closed and secured, and the Austrians were driven away definitively on the left, where, in a little less than two hours nearly, four hundred prisoners were taken.

It was in this last phase of combat that Corridoni met his death.

After having withstood for a long time the assault of massive enemy forces that were attempting to chase us from the trench, under the crossfire of rifles and artillery, poor Pippo had had his men construct a defensive traverse, and doggedly resisted. On every other point as well, the resistance was heroic! When reinforcements came to fortify our positions, Corridoni greeted them with rapture.

Eye witnesses told me that he greeted them by waving his beret joyfully and crying out "Victory, Victory!" It was at that moment that an enemy bullet reached him, hitting him in the forehead. The volunteer Pandolfini tried to hold him up, but a new projectile, perhaps fired by the same murderous weapon, struck him in the left arm, immediately immobilizing him. He bent over the body of his poor friend, and confirmed his death, which was instantaneous from the discharge of cerebral mass.

Apotheosis

Thus, with the great dream in his heart, absorbed in that magnificent vision of Victory, Filippo Corridoni gave his young life on the Carso, struck down by a bullet in the forehead, in the conquered trench.

The ancient Greeks had an endearing phrase for depicting so noble and worthy an ending: *Eutanasia*, which means "the beautiful death." I am certain that, if he could have chosen, he would have chosen the fate that befell him.

Indeed, he had said not too long before [his death]: "I will die in a hole, against a rock, or in the fury of an assault; but – if I can – I will fall with my face toward the enemy, as if to go further forward still."

To him, deceased, an apotheosis has been decreed. His heroic end resonated widely in all of Italy. And it was not only those who had known him and loved him who wept for him. Those even who had persecuted and dishonored him when he was fighting his civic battles, mistaking him for a demagogue in pursuit of popularity, felt compelled to bow before his tomb, which shines like an altar, even if the place where he was buried remains unknown.

Such is the fate of men like Filippo Corridoni: they need to die, that justice might be rendered them.

The Fatherland recognized too late – just as King Lear had with Cordelia in Shakespeare – just what a pure, ardent, profound affection, even if not outwardly shown, this its child bore for her, towards whom it had been prodigal only with handcuffs and prisons.

The revolutionary ten times sentenced for antimilitarism died in the "trenches of the fronds" wearing the gray-green uniform, as if he had died on a barricade, for the Cause which was the love and pangs of his entire tormented existence: the renewal of Italy, liberated at that very moment from every foreign oppression or control, as from every internal tyranny. The same generous fever, the same never-satiated thirst for justice and sacrifice that had driven him to the front line of labor strikes, and into street revolts, to prison and into exile – had led him to the war and made a hero of him.

Other Books by the Publisher

Fanchette's Pretty Little Foot by Restif de la Bretonne

Je M'Accuse... by Léon Bloy

My Hospitals & My Prisons by Paul Verlaine

Salvation Through the Jews by Léon Bloy

Words of a Demolitions Contractor by Léon Bloy

Cellulely by Paul Verlaine

Ecclesiastical Laurels by Jacques Rochette de la Morlière

Flowers of Bitumen by Émile Goudeau

Songs for Her & Odes in Her Honor by Paul Verlaine

On Huysmans' Tomb by Léon Bloy

Ten Years a Bohemian by Émile Goudeau

The Soul of Napoleon by Léon Bloy

Blood of the Poor by Léon Bloy

Joan of Arc and Germany by Léon Bloy

A Platonic Love by Paul Alexis

The Revealer of the Globe: Christopher Columbus & His Future Beatification (Part One) by Léon Bloy

An Immodest Proposal by Dr. Helmut Schleppend

The Pornographer by Restif de la Bretonne

Style (Theory and History) by Ernest Hello

On the Threshold of the Apocalypse: 1913-1915 by Léon Bloy

She Who Weeps (Our Lady of La Salette) by Léon Bloy

The Sylph by Claude Prosper Jolyot de Crébillon (*fils*)

Voyage in France by a Frenchman by Paul Verlaine

Ourigan, Oregon by William Clark, Richard Robinson, and anonymous

Drowning by Yu Dafu

Cull of April by Francis Vielé-Griffin

The Misfortune of Monsieur Fraque by Paul Alexis

Fêtes Galantes & Songs Without Words by Paul Verlaine

Joys by Francis Vielé-Griffin

The Son of Louis XVI by Léon Bloy

Septentrion by Jean Raspail

The Resurrection of Villiers de l'Isle-Adam by Léon Bloy

Poems Saturnian by Paul Verlaine

The Biography of Léon Bloy: Memories of a Friend by René Martineau

Fredegund, France: A Book of Poetry by Richard Robinson

The Good Song by Paul Verlaine

Swans by Francis Vielé-Griffin

Constantinople and Byzantium by Léon Bloy

Fallacies: Part 3, Book 4 of Summa Logicae by William of Ockham

What Is Fascism by Sergio Panunzio